MW00909775

NIMBOSTRATUS

STRATOCUMULUS

CUMULUS

CUMULONIMBUS

STRATUS

To Aaron Thornberry — July 5, 1990 — from Virginia + Jim

WEATHER

By Howard E. Smith, Jr.
Illustrated by Jeffrey K. Bedrick

DOUBLEDAY   NEW YORK LONDON TORONTO SYDNEY AUCKLAND

Published by Doubleday, a division of
Bantam Doubleday Dell Publishing
Group, Inc., 666 Fifth Avenue,
New York, New York 10103

Doubleday and the portrayal of an
anchor with a dolphin are trademarks of
Doubleday, a division of Bantam
Doubleday Dell Publishing Group, Inc.

Library of Congress
Cataloging-in-Publication Data
Smith, Howard Everett, 1927–
    Weather / by Howard E. Smith;
illustrated by Jeffrey Bedrick.
        p.   cm.
    Summary: Text and illustrations
introduce weather, including tornadoes,
fog, heat, and future climate.
    1. Weather—Juvenile literature.
[1. Weather.] I. Bedrick, Jeffrey, ill.
II. Title. QC981.3.S63 1990
551.5—dc19   89-1111 CIP   AC
ISBN 0-385-26085-7
        0-385-26086-5 (lib. bdg.)
RL: 3.7
Text copyright © 1990
by Howard E. Smith, Jr.
Illustrations copyright © 1990
by Jeffrey Bedrick
All Rights Reserved
Printed in Singapore
May 1990
First Edition

To place a credit card order of $25.00 or
more, call toll-free 1-800-223-6834, Ext.
9479. In New York, please call 1-212-
492-9479. Or send your order, plus
$2.00 for shipping and handling, to the
following address: Doubleday Readers
Service, Dept. FM, P.O. Box 5071, Des
Plaines, IL 60017-5071. Prices and
availability are subject to change
without notice. Please allow four to six
weeks for delivery.

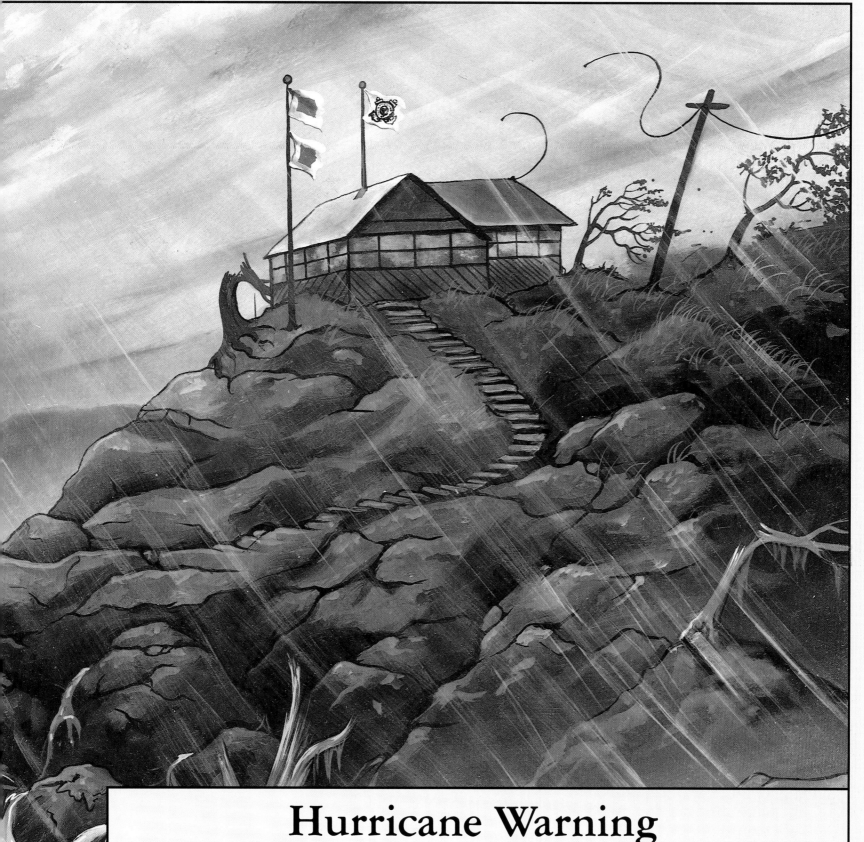

Hurricane Warning

Hurricane warning flags fly at Coast Guard stations along the coast. Radio weather forecasts announce that a storm is close. People nervously prepare for the worst. Many nail wooden shutters or boards over their windows. For safety, those near the seacoast leave the area.

The great winds arrive. Sheets of rain pour down. Giant waves start breaking up piers. Boats that are smashed by waves sink. Trees fall, trapping and killing people. Telephone and electric wires snap. Houses and other buildings collapse, and more people are killed. The full force of a hurricane is at work.

How Does a Hurricane Develop?

In spite of great efforts and millions of dollars spent on research, no one knows exactly how a hurricane gets started. But we do know that during the summer and early autumn months, the constantly flowing warm trade winds, blowing from the northeast in the South Atlantic, become disturbed when cold air masses from the north pass them. The crosswinds often form tropical storms.

If you could see all of such a storm, it would resemble an enormous doughnut up to hundreds of miles wide. Clouds might at times rise 60,000 feet high. The storm would have a small hollow place in its center, which is called the eye of the storm.

Winds of tropical storms move in a typical pattern. Warm, damp air from the sun-heated tropical ocean water rises up inside of the eye several miles high. As it does, it cools; raindrops

form and then fall. This newly cooled air rides up over the top and outside surface of the doughnut-shaped storm and falls down its sides. This falling cool air puts pressure on the warm sea air, forcing it back up inside the eye of the storm. This cycle continues, and the storm soon resembles a tremendously large and powerful heat engine, which continually pumps up warm air.

Not all tropical storms keep going. Cool air over land or cool ocean currents can break them up. A storm always breaks up if it goes over a land area, such as Florida or Cuba. If, however, a storm continues, it becomes larger. Some grow to be hundreds of miles in diameter. Wind speeds increase, going, in some storms, over 74 miles per hour. Once winds hit 74 miles per hour or higher, the storm is called a hurricane. But the winds often don't stop increasing at that speed. In some hurricanes, winds have reached 200 miles per hour. The winds are strongest near the eye. Oddly enough, the air inside the eye is calm, with nothing more than gentle breezes.

Many rain clouds appear in a hurricane. They form arc-shaped concentric bands around the center of the storm. Torrents of rain fall from

them. Fierce thunderstorms appear. Hail often falls. Tornadoes or waterspouts, or both, may appear. Waterspouts are actually tornadoes that appear over open water. Tons of water are sucked up into them. Though not as dangerous as tornadoes, waterspouts can sink small ships.

A hurricane not only rotates around the eye, it also moves along a storm path. No one ever knows where a hurricane will go—Bermuda, the Caribbean islands, Mexico, the Atlantic or Gulf coast of the United States. A few fierce ones, such as Hurricane Carol and Hurricane Hazel, have even reached Canada.

Many methods are used to track hurricanes. Sensors on satellites circling the earth, hundreds of miles above the oceans, detect cloud formations that could develop into hurricanes. Radar follows the storms. To keep track of them, airplanes fly above them.

Once a dangerous tropical storm is found, the U.S. National Weather Service will broadcast its location. When it heads for a shoreline area, warnings will be issued. If it turns into a hurricane, then hurricane warnings will be issued. Hurricane flags will be flown at Coast Guard stations. This international signal is two square red flags with black squares in the middle, flying one above the other.

To be safe, listen to warnings. These warnings are always broadcast hours, or sometimes even days, before a hurricane strikes. Follow the directions of authorities. Take in lawn furniture, trash cans, and other objects that might blow around and hit or cut people. Also board up or tape windows to keep them from shattering. If you are caught in the high winds, beware of objects flying in the air and seek shelter in a strong building on high land. Stay away from windows. Beware of falling trees and broken power lines. They can electrocute you.

Only the tropical storms of the Atlantic Ocean are called hurricanes. In the Pacific they are called "typhoons," "cyclones," or "willy-willies."

In spite of their terrible power for destruction, hurricanes are not all bad. They bring much-needed rains from the tropics to the temperate zones. Without this moisture, North America would, for example, grow much less wheat and corn.

Which Hurricanes Were the Worst?

The great Galveston, Texas, hurricane of September 8, 1900, has no equal. Over 6,000 people were killed. This was, in terms of deaths, by far the worst natural disaster North Americans have ever faced.

In low-lying Galveston, huge waves easily swept over the city and drowned thousands. Waves and wind battered down buildings, and even ripped away heavy coastal defense cannons. After the storm, unbelievable destruction and dead people could be seen everywhere. To stop the spread of diseases, U.S. Army troops burned hundreds of corpses in huge bonfires.

A typhoon that struck Bangladesh in 1970 rates as the worst windstorm in modern times. High winds pushed seawater over very low-lying lands in Bangladesh. Over one million people were killed; almost all of them drowned in water that was just over their heads. Everywhere, towns, fields, crops lay in ruins.

Wind

The wind is caused by the uneven heating of the earth by the sun. Cold air is heavier and more dense than warm air. Cold, dry air is the heaviest of all. Warm, humid air is least dense, and so it will rise above cold air. Whenever it does, cold air moves in under it. Whenever this happens, a wind blows.

You can tell how fast the wind is blowing by the Beaufort Scale.

THE BEAUFORT SCALE

MILES PER HOUR	ON LAND
0–1	Smoke rises vertically
1–3	Smoke drifts slowly
4–7	Leaves rustle
8–12	Twigs are in motion
13–18	Small branches move
19–24	Small trees sway
25–31	Large branches sway
32–38	Whole trees are in motion
39–46	Twigs break off
47–54	Branches break
55–63	Trees snap or bow down
64–72	Widespread damage
73–plus	Extreme damage

MILES PER HOUR	ON THE SEA
0–3	Sea calm
8	Parts of surface wind-ruffled
13	All the surface ruffled
18	A few whitecaps
23	About half of wave tops have whitecaps
28	All wave tops have whitecaps
34–48	Spray blows off whitecaps
48–56	High waves, breaking at crests
56 and up	Wave tops blown away

Air Masses

Cold air and warm air usually form into large air masses. These huge air masses often cover tens of thousands of square miles. Most recurring air masses have names. The coldest air mass in the United States (excluding Alaska) is the Siberian. It develops in Siberia and may actually cross over the north pole itself and move down across the Canadian border, bringing record cold weather. The Gulf air mass is a very warm and humid air mass that originates over the Gulf of Mexico. In the summer it brings stifling hot weather to the United States. In the winter it brings gray, wet weather. The North Pacific air mass is cool and damp. It brings heavy rains to the Northwest and sometimes all the way east to the Atlantic coast.

Most Canadian air masses are the
same as those of the United States. Yet
the one that comes up into Canada
from the Gulf and Midwest is called
the Tropical air mass in Canada.
Australian air masses are the Indian
Tropical, Pacific Tropical, Subpolar
Maritime, and Indian and Pacific
Subtropical. England also has names for
its air masses. Three are very cold: the
Arctic Maritime, which comes straight
down from the north; the Arctic
Continental, which comes from Russia;
and the Polar Continental, which comes
from Siberia. A moderate air mass, the
Polar Maritime, comes from North
America. Two warm masses move over
England: the Tropic Continental, which
comes from the Sahara Desert, and
Tropical Maritime from the tropical
zone of the Atlantic.

No air mass stays still for more than
a few days at a time. Each is constantly
on the move. Their motions are what
bring us changes in the weather. By
keeping track of the motion of air
masses, weather services all over the
world can better predict the weather.

When Air Masses Meet

When air masses meet, the weather changes. In fact, when they meet, rain or snow almost always falls or high winds start blowing.

When a moving warm air mass meets a cold air mass we have a warm front. When it meets a stationary cold air mass and keeps moving, it usually slips up over it. This happens because warm, damp air is lighter than cold air, and so it "floats" on top of the cooler air. When it does, certain clouds appear. First, cirrus clouds appear. They are often called "mares' tails" for they look sort of like long, slender horsetails. Next, cirrocumulus appear. These form into groups of small clouds called a "mackerel sky" because they look like the scales of that fish. These clouds thicken and form altostratus clouds, which are uniformly dark and gray. Rain or snow falls from altostratus clouds as they thicken further. The whole cycle from clear weather to rain usually takes two or three days or

longer, but may take less than a day. After it rains for hours or days, the clouds break up and the sun appears. The weather will be warm or even hot and humid.

When a cold air mass advances, we have a cold front. When a fast-moving cold air mass collides with a warm air mass, the cold air, being heavier than the warm, humid air, will move under the warm air mass. As it does, it will rapidly lift the warm, damp air to great heights. In that case cumulus clouds called thunderheads will appear. These thunderheads often resemble cauliflower heads.

Severe thunderstorms may follow, with lightning and heavy downpours. On occasion, hailstorms may occur, tornadoes may form, or both may occur together.

After the cold air mass passes, the rain stops, the sky clears, and dry cool or cold weather follows. Some of the best dry and clear weather is found after these thunderstorms.

In winter, snowstorms or blizzards may occur when a cold front lifts a warm front. After the storm, calm, crisp, cold air and bright days will follow.

Fog and Smog

Sometimes fog settles in after a warm front moves by. Fog is a low-lying cloud. The drops of water in it are actually too small and lightweight to fall to the ground. Because the slightest updrafts can lift them, most never make it to the ground. Though calm and at times beautiful, fog is dangerous, especially on roads and highways where it has caused many fatal accidents.

At sea, fog is equally bad. One of the worst disasters caused by fog took place July 25, 1956, when two beautiful ocean liners, the *Andrea Doria* and the *Stockholm*, collided in fog not far from Nantucket Island. Fifty-one people were killed, and the luxurious *Andrea Doria* sank.

Smog is related to fog. It is a part natural and part man-made weather condition that occurs with or without fog, during very calm weather.

Dangerous particles from chemicals or from burning coal or oil gather in the air. The most dangerous are the nitrous and sulfur compounds, because they harm people's eyes and lungs. In addition, visibility drops, even to the point where people cannot see where they are going.

In December of 1952, a terrible smog combined with fog held London, England, in its grip. People couldn't see where they were going. Many pedestrians got hopelessly lost, and some froze to death. A few died falling down steps; others fell into the Thames River and drowned. Most, however, died of lung failure, caused primarily by bronchitis or asthma. The death toll reached 3,500. Because of this treacherous smog, the city of London banned the burning of coal and certain types of oil. Since then the air has become much cleaner and is far safer.

In a smog, one should, if possible, leave town. Otherwise close windows, stay indoors, and remain as inactive as possible.

Thunderstorms

Thunderstorms start as tall cumulus clouds of heated air surge upward in cooler surrounding air, which happens when a cold front meets a warm air mass and lifts it. These clouds, often called thunderheads, are some of the tallest clouds ever seen, sometimes reaching over 60,000 feet in elevation—over eleven miles high!

Lightning, which usually accompanies a thunderstorm, is nothing more than an enormous electric spark, but it has awesome power. The electric current in an average household carries 15 amperes of electricity. An ampere is a measure of the amount of current. Yet a lightning stroke can carry 200,000 amperes! A single large lightning stroke could power all the electrical needs of the state of Arizona or the city of Melbourne, Australia. A big stroke may carry 30 million volts. A volt measures the force of an electric current. Most houses are powered by 110 volts of electricity.

What causes these powerful lightning strokes? No one knows everything about how they come into being. Since lightning is an electrical spark, particles in the air must somehow become charged with electricity to create the spark. But how?

We know that objects rubbing against each other can produce electricity. For example, we sometimes pick up electrical charges from walking on carpets and get sparks from a metal doorknob on cold, dry winter days.

Particles in the air get charged in a similar way. Experts think that as particles move rapidly in the air they collect electric charges, in the form of electrons, from other particles in the air. Raindrops in thunderstorms move at great speeds, gaining or losing electrons as they rush and rub against one another.

For an unknown reason, inside of a cloud the plus, or positive, charges gather near the top of a cloud, the minus, or negative, charges at middle levels of the cloud, and plus charges again at lower levels. Most lightning strokes take place inside a cloud between plus and minus charges. Lightning also jumps from one cloud to another. Some strokes go over twenty miles from one cloud to another. But at other times, the lower levels of a cloud attract charges in the ground far below the cloud.

Sometimes, before lightning strikes, one sees the weird "Saint Elmo's fire." Objects glow with a strange blue light. Your hair may actually stand on end. Odd electric, hairy-looking blue flames reach upward. Sometimes metal objects, such as fire escapes, "sing" with a whiny hum. When this happens, lightning will almost always strike.

We think we see lightning strike downward from the cloud to the ground or to tall objects. Yet just before we see the stroke, several things happen. First a faintly seen electrical current, called a leader, moves downward from the cloud. This "jumps" in 50-yard "leaps" toward the ground. It makes each 50-yard jump in a mere 50 millionth of a second. The hot core of this leader is only about

half an inch in diameter, but we see the larger, glowing hot light that surrounds it. When it gets almost to the ground, a far larger lightning stroke leaps upward from the ground toward the cloud, following the path of the leader. This stroke may be 20 feet in diameter. It moves up to half the speed of light, at between 60,000 and 90,000 miles per second! It is tremendously hot—up to about 50,000 degrees Fahrenheit. That's five times the temperature found on the surface of the sun. These up and down strokes happen too fast for us to see them. What we think is one stroke may be five or so.

Contrary to popular myth, lightning often strikes the same place over and over again.

The incredibly hot lightning instantly heats up and expands the air around it. Then the surrounding cool air, replacing it, slams together at speeds above the speed of sound. What we hear as thunder is actually an enormous sonic boom. Some thunder is so loud that it can be heard 18 miles away.

Lightning can be very dangerous. Always be careful in a lightning storm. Don't be near a lone tall tree or even a small group of trees. The interior of a forest, however, is quite safe. If you are swimming, get out of the water, because it conducts electricity. Don't be outdoors if you can help it. If you are in a house stay away from metal objects such as radiators, telephones, or wires because they conduct electricity. Keep the windows closed. If you are in a car with all the windows shut, you are very safe. This is so because the rubber tires are insulators and break contact with the ground.

Hailstorms

Hail usually accompanies thunderstorms. Hailstones begin as raindrops. First raindrops fall inside the mid-regions of towering thunderheads. But strong updrafts, sometimes moving over a hundred miles an hour, can easily push the raindrops up to higher levels where the air is exceptionally cold, sometimes reaching temperatures of minus 40 degrees F. There, high up in the thunderheads, the raindrops freeze and so turn to hail.

The largest hailstone ever measured fell in Kansas in 1970. It was 7 1/2 inches across and weighed 1.67 pounds. Severe hailstorms pose a constant threat to farmers, because they ruin crops. They also dent car roofs, break greenhouse roofs and, on extremely rare occasions, kill people. If you are caught in the open in a hailstorm and cannot find shelter, put your hands over your head or put something such as a folded coat over it.

Tornadoes

When tornadoes appear, they almost always accompany severe thunderstorms. Experts believe that tornadoes start when a layer of wind above the ground moves faster than the wind near the ground. This causes the faster-moving wind to roll the slower-moving wind under it, much as you would roll a tin can under your hand. A cylinder-shaped roll of wind can be miles long.

The strong updraft in a thunderstorm may raise the rolling wind up to a vertical position. At the same time, the whirling winds may force a wheel-shaped cloud in the thunderstorm to rotate. This cloud, called a mesocyclone, gives power to a tornado as it begins to form.

A long-lived tornado may travel for over a hundred miles. Even so, all tornadoes are soon doomed. The cool air surrounding a tornado will eventually pinch in on its sides and destroy it.

No storm on earth equals a tornado for ferocity. Its winds have been clocked at 230 miles per hour, but studies show a tornado's winds can hit at least 260 miles per hour.

Some people have actually looked up into the funnel of a tornado and lived to tell about it. They say that it is mostly dark up there, but constant strokes of flickering lightning light up its insides. The roar in the funnel is said to be weird, something like the sound of a thousand freight trains.

During the time when heavy thunderstorms are about, or when there are disturbing weather conditions, listen to the radio or television for tornado warnings. The National Severe Storms Center in Kansas City, Kansas, will issue what is called a tornado advisory which indicates that a tornado may occur. If the Center spots a tornado with its radar and communications systems or if anyone reports a tornado, the Center determines its likely path and immediately issues a tornado warning. At the same time, people in areas where the tornado might strike may also be warned by warning sirens.

Once you hear a radio warning or the sirens, take immediate cover. The best cover is a prepared storm shelter. The second-best is the basement of a frame house. Go into the basement and crouch down under a sturdy table on the opposite side of the room from the direction from which the tornado is approaching. Tornadoes blow debris away from this side. If you don't know how an approaching tornado is moving, go to the southwest corner, as tornadoes usually move from the southwest to the northeast.

Opening windows does no good. Don't waste time with them. Do not use the basement of a stone or brick house as a shelter, as the collapsing heavy materials could crush or trap you.

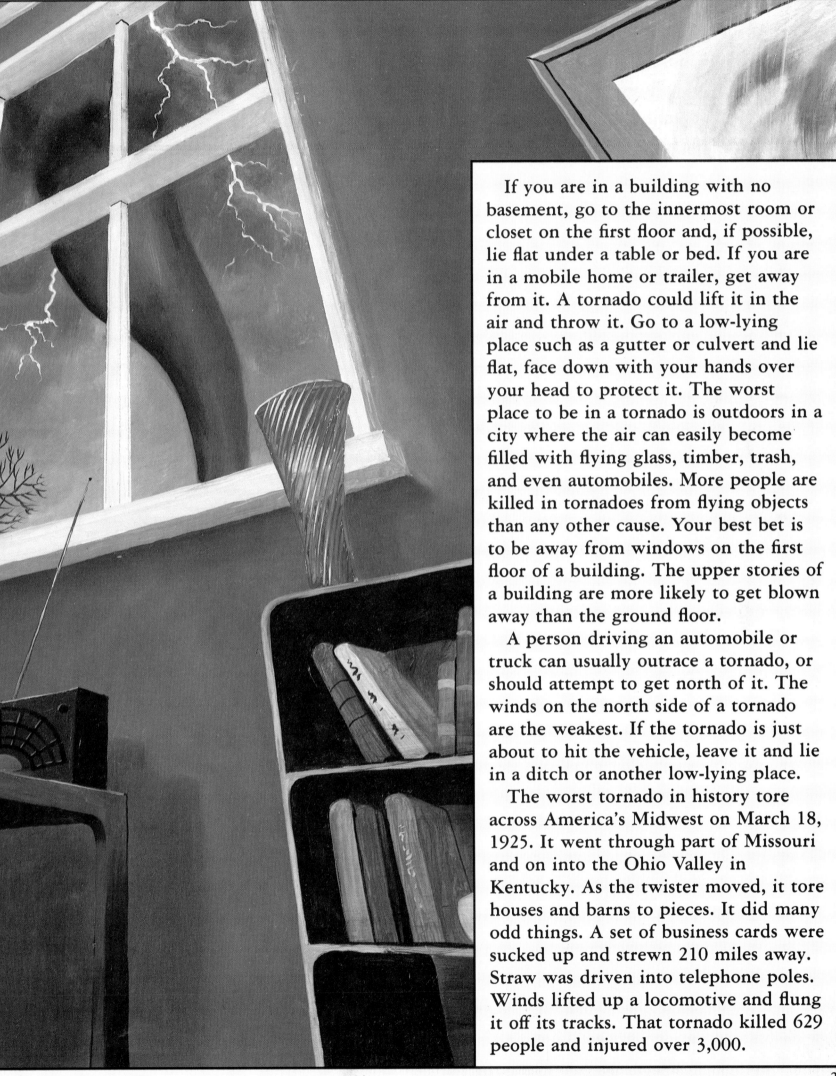

If you are in a building with no basement, go to the innermost room or closet on the first floor and, if possible, lie flat under a table or bed. If you are in a mobile home or trailer, get away from it. A tornado could lift it in the air and throw it. Go to a low-lying place such as a gutter or culvert and lie flat, face down with your hands over your head to protect it. The worst place to be in a tornado is outdoors in a city where the air can easily become filled with flying glass, timber, trash, and even automobiles. More people are killed in tornadoes from flying objects than any other cause. Your best bet is to be away from windows on the first floor of a building. The upper stories of a building are more likely to get blown away than the ground floor.

A person driving an automobile or truck can usually outrace a tornado, or should attempt to get north of it. The winds on the north side of a tornado are the weakest. If the tornado is just about to hit the vehicle, leave it and lie in a ditch or another low-lying place.

The worst tornado in history tore across America's Midwest on March 18, 1925. It went through part of Missouri and on into the Ohio Valley in Kentucky. As the twister moved, it tore houses and barns to pieces. It did many odd things. A set of business cards were sucked up and strewn 210 miles away. Straw was driven into telephone poles. Winds lifted up a locomotive and flung it off its tracks. That tornado killed 629 people and injured over 3,000.

Rainfall

Rainfall is caused by temperature differences in humid air. No doubt on a hot, damp day you've watched drops of water form on the outside of a cold glass of ice and water. The drops form because there is water vapor in the air surrounding the glass. When the warm air touches the surface of the glass and cools, the vapor condenses into water drops.

Clouds form when invisible water vapor in the air cools down enough to form tiny droplets. When the air cools further, the drops in the clouds become larger. When they become large enough, they will fall as rain.

Some places are exceptionally rainy, especially sea islands and mountains. This is so because when warm, damp sea breezes hit islands, and especially mountains, they often cool down so that rains form. Much of New Zealand, for example, is rainy for this reason.

The rainiest place on earth in terms of days of rain is Mount Waialeale on the island of Kauai, Hawaii. There it rains an average of 335 days per year. Usually about 450 inches of rain fall each year. The greatest amount of rain in a year fell in Cherrapunji, Assam. From August 1, 1860 to July 31, 1861, 1041.78 inches of rain fell.

The rainiest city in the continental United States is Mobile, Alabama, which has an average rainfall of 66.98 inches per year. The rainiest places in the British Isles are in the mountains of Scotland, Wales, and England. Two

hundred inches of rain a year sometimes falls in these places, making them the wettest in Europe. The heaviest rainfall in New Zealand was at Homer Tunnel in 1940 when 380.7 inches fell there in a year.

Sometimes there are terrible "cloudbursts," which are short-lived but severe rains. In one minute at Unionville, Maryland, on July 4, 1956, 1.23 inches of rain fell, which is a world record. The worst such rainfall in the world was at Cilaos, Isle de Réunion, in the Indian Ocean where 73.62 inches fell in twenty-four hours on March 16, 1952.

Floods occur when snows melt or during and after heavy rains. The worst flood in history took place on the Yellow River in China in August, 1931. An estimated 3,700,000 people died because of the raging floodwaters.

In the U.S.A. more people are killed in flash floods than in any other type of storm. These dangerous storms frequently occur in deserts or mountains all over the world. In many mountain and desert canyons, one is likely to see signs warning that an area is subject to flash floods. In deserts, people are told not to camp in certain areas or cross dry riverbeds if there is a rainstorm in the area. In mountainous areas, people are told to leave their cars or camps and immediately climb up high on canyon walls.

Flash floods occur when a brief but intense rainfall takes place and water rises very rapidly in streambeds in narrow canyons. The rain does not always fall where the flood occurs but may fall ten or more miles upstream from the flood area.

The opposite of the wettest places are, of course, the driest places. In the United States the driest place is Death Valley, in eastern California and southern Nevada. Many years not a drop of water falls. Yet in some years cloudbursts flood parts of the area. The Atacama Desert of South America is the driest desert on earth. For four hundred years no rain fell there! Then oddly, rains fell in 1971. The driest place in the Australian Desert is near Lake Eyre. This region gets 5 inches of rain a year on an average. Canada's driest area is in the northernmost Arctic islands, which average a mere 3.9 inches per year.

Droughts occur when yearly rains fail. The worst drought in America took place in the 1930s. The American plains turned into what people called the Dust Bowl. Dust storms made up of huge clouds of dust blew from Nebraska toward the east, some going to New York City, some to Washington, D.C., and some even onto ships far out in the Atlantic Ocean.

Dust storms bury fields, even houses, and when dust gets into the working parts of machines, it can destroy them. Moreover, dust gets into people's food, underclothing, ears and noses—everywhere. Occasionally people become lost in dust storms and, on very rare occasions, die. Perhaps worst of all, dust storms generate electricity in the air. This electricity greatly disturbs people, making them feel nervous and often excitable or depressed. In addition, dust storms often carry harmful fungi and bacteria that cause sicknesses. During the Dust Bowl years of the 1930s, crops failed on the plains. Farmers gave up and abandoned their homes, their fields, and migrated out of the region. As people lost farms and wages, this terrible drought made the Great Depression worse.

The drought of 1968–75 in the Sahel, an area just south of the Sahara Desert in Africa, was one of the worst in history. Countless nomadic people were forced to give up their way of life. Hundreds of thousands of people died; of these, great numbers were herders of the desert who died lonely deaths on the sands. Because families split up and took animals to separate pastures, many never found their families again. Cities became overcrowded, diseases spread like wildfire. No one knows what the death toll was, but at least 500,000 people died.

Snow and Blizzards

A snowflake forms its six-pointed, icy lacework around one or more tiny dust particles. No two snowflakes look exactly alike because each snowflake has its own history. As a flake falls, it constantly gathers extra ice and dust, which shape it. As it collides with other flakes it either gets damaged by them or sticks to them, again changing its shape.

The severest snowstorms are blizzards. A blizzard is defined by the U.S. National Weather Service as a condition when winds are 35 mph or higher, the temperature is 20 degrees F. or lower, and snow, either blown from the ground or falling, reduces visibility to a quarter of a mile or less. A severe blizzard is defined as having winds of 45 mph or higher, a temperature of 10 degrees F. or lower, and near zero visibility. In all blizzards, winds form snowdrifts. Blizzards can shut highways, stop trains, and bring life in a big city to a halt. Motorists stuck in blizzards may freeze to death.

Occasionally people become buried in drifts, not to be found again for weeks.

The greatest one-day snowfall ever recorded took place at Silver Lake, Colorado: 76 inches of snow fell in twenty-four hours from April 14 to 15, 1921. During a twelve-month period, from February 19, 1971, to February 18, 1972, 1,224.5 inches fell at Paradise, Mount Rainier, in Washington.

Year in and year out, the deepest winter snows in the world fall in the Sierra Nevada Mountains and Cascade Mountains of California, Oregon, and Washington. This is so because moisture-filled clouds moving west to east from the Pacific Ocean rise over these Pacific Coast mountains and dump their snow on them. Canada has deep snows—72 feet fell in one year at Kildala Pass, British Columbia. So does England; in a single 56-hour storm, 42 inches of snow fell at Durham in February 1941.

Though there is ice in mile-deep glaciers in Antarctica and the Arctic, these regions, odd as it may seem, get much less snow. In fact, they are actually desert regions. The ice, much of which never melts, is deep because it has accumulated over hundreds of thousands of years.

The Heat and the Cold

Year in and year out, some places on earth become terribly cold. As one might suspect, the coldest temperatures ever recorded on earth were taken in Antarctica. At a place in the middle of Antarctica (78 South Latitude and 96 East Longitude) the annual mean temperature was minus 72 degrees F. An annual mean temperature is exactly halfway between the highest and lowest yearly recordings.

The coldest temperature recorded in England was minus 17 degrees F. at Braemar, Aberdeen, on February 11, 1895. In Australia it was 7.6 degrees F. at Charlotte Pass, on July 14, 1945. In New Zealand it was minus 3.5 degrees F. at Ophir, on July 2, 1943. In Canada it was minus 81 degrees F. at Snag, in the Yukon, on February 3, 1947. The lowest temperature in Alaska was minus 95 degrees F. on Mount McKinley (this might have been lower —the thermometer broke) and minus 79.9 degrees F. on January 23, 1971, at a town called Prospect Creek Camp. The lowest temperature for states in the U.S.A. south of Canada was minus 70 degrees F. on January 20, 1954, at Rodgers Pass, Montana.

The lowest recorded temperature in the world was at Vostok, Antarctica, at minus 129 degrees F. on July 21, 1983. The coldest inhabited town in the world is Omyakon, Siberia, where the temperature has plunged to minus 96 degrees F.

The hottest place on earth is Dallol, Ethiopia, which had an annual mean temperature of 95 degrees F. from 1960 to 1966. The hottest temperature ever recorded was 136.4 degrees F. in Al'Aziziyah, Libya, on September 13, 1922.

The place with the least temperature variation in the world is Saipan, an island in the Pacific Ocean where the temperature remains year-round, night and day, between 67 and 85 degrees F.

The hottest place in the United States is Death Valley, where the temperature has reached 134 degrees F. The hottest temperature in Canada was 112 degrees F. at Emerson, Manitoba, on July 12, 1936; in Australia it was 128 degrees F. at Cloncurry, Queensland, January 16, 1889; in New Zealand it was 101.2 degrees F. at Ashburton, January 19, 1956; in England it was 100.5 degrees F. at Tunbridge, Kent, on July 22, 1868.

In the U.S.A., San Francisco, California, has the least variation in temperature. The monthly normal temperature varies only from 48 degrees F. in January to 64 degrees F. in September. An equitable climate such as that of San Francisco is called a Mediterranean climate. In such a climate it rarely freezes in the winter and summers are long and dry. In the winter it rains. Such a climate, of course, was named after that found in Spain, Italy, Greece and parts of north Africa at or close to the Mediterranean Sea. It is also found in Turkey, south of the Caspian Sea, in Chile, southwestern South Africa, southwestern Australia, and parts of New Zealand.

Scientists Explore Ancient Climates

Most scientists define climates as long-term weather patterns lasting at least thirty-five years, but they can last for centuries. It seems as though it would be impossible for us to know about climate conditions in the past, but scientists know a great deal about past climates and are finding out more all the time. How do they do it?

One way is to examine the tree rings of ancient trees. Trees grow thicker annual rings during wet years, and thinner annual rings during dry years. By examining tree rings in the United States, scientists know about yearly dry or wet weather patterns going back about two thousand years.

Other scientists have examined ice cores of glaciers. These are obtained by means of special drills that bring up cylinder-shaped cores from deep in the ice. Ice cores brought up from glaciers in Greenland and the Antarctic show climate patterns going back a million years.

Fossils, too, tell scientists much about the climate tens and even hundreds of millions of years ago. For example, since coral can only grow in warm seas, the presence of fossil corals shows that the climate was warm where they are found. Since dragonflies can only live in warm, damp places, their fossils indicate a warm climate in the past. On the other hand, glacial scars on rocks, which glaciers left when the rocks they were carrying rubbed against them, show ancient cold climates.

Today there is great interest in a huge comet or asteroid that may have struck the earth about 65 million years ago. When it hit, huge dust clouds would have risen into the air and blocked sunlight for months or years and cooled down the earth. This could have killed off the dinosaurs by lowering the earth's temperature, chilling or freezing them, and preventing the growth of types of vegetation that they needed.

Future Climates

Scientists are greatly interested in future climates. Right now, their attention is focused on the so-called "greenhouse effect." This term refers to the way the earth's atmosphere traps heat. Just as the glass in greenhouses keeps heat in, so certain gases, primarily carbon dioxide (CO_2), can trap heat in the atmosphere. Unfortunately, in today's world automobiles and smokestacks give off too much carbon dioxide, which many scientists believe is trapping too much heat in the earth's atmosphere and overheating the earth.

Recent measurements show that the 1980s were the warmest decade in over a century. In the summer of 1988 the plains states and southeastern United States suffered from a severe drought accompanied by record-breaking heat waves.

During this severe summer, valuable wheat, barley, corn, and soybean crops were destroyed. Moreover, the level of the mighty Mississippi River dropped so much that barge traffic stopped.

This drought and its accompanying heat waves convinced most scientists that the world is heating up—primarily because of the emission of huge quantities of carbon dioxide and, to a lesser degree, other gases. Congress decided to act, and set up a committee to study the problem. In June of 1988, James Hansen of NASA became a star witness in a Senate hearing. He stated that scientists were sure that the "greenhouse effect had been detected."

In Toronto, the Canadian government set up a conference called the "Conference on the Changing Atmosphere." Three hundred science experts from forty-eight countries attended.

Other scientists, however, think that normal, recurring changes in tropical ocean currents brought about the heat waves and drought in the summer of 1988. Only time will tell which theory is correct.

At any rate, in the next century there will be problems in parts of the world if, as many scientists expect, the earth grows warmer. Deserts will spread, particularly in America. Los Angeles will be far drier, and its population far less. Many important crops, such as wheat and corn, will be grown farther north in new areas. Many American cities will be hotter. For example, New York City now has an average of fifteen days a year when the temperature goes above 90 degrees F.; in A.D. 2030 it will have forty-eight such days. All cities in temperate zone areas, such as England and parts of Australia and New Zealand, will see similar increases.

Under the worst conditions, the earth could possibly warm up by 20 degrees F. by 2075. Most likely it will warm up by 5 to 10 degrees F., which is still too much.

If the earth continues to warm up, glaciers will partly melt and their water will flow into the oceans. This will make the oceans rise. By the year 2050, oceans will be four feet higher. Parts of London and New York City will be under water. If all the glaciers melt, three fourths of Florida will be underwater; so will all low-lying areas of England and, for example, Belgium and Holland.

Would all the news be bad? Not necessarily. For good news, there will be many fewer droughts in East Africa. The Soviet Union, Scandinavia, Canada, and cooler regions of southern temperate zones in New Zealand and Tasmania will benefit from longer growing seasons.

What can be done to stop the greenhouse effect? The less fuel burned in factories, the less carbon dioxide will be produced. We may have to give up many luxury items. Automobiles should be designed to get many more miles to the gallon of gas. Buildings should be better insulated so that less fuel will be needed to heat them.

Urban planners should plan cities designed for less congestion. Huge amounts of gasoline are burned by automobiles just waiting in traffic! Even more efficient light bulbs would be a big help. By using more solar or wind or nuclear energy instead of oil, gas, coal, or wood, people in the future could lessen the greenhouse effect. Since trees and other plants use carbon dioxide, and in the process clean the air and also give off oxygen, many more trees should be planted. All efforts should be made to stop the current uncontrolled cutting of forest and jungle areas. This destruction rates as an ecological and atmospheric disaster.

Could another Ice Age be in the making? Possibly. Though right now the world's climate is warming up, and will for at least a century or more, this does not mean that an Ice Age, thousands of years off in the future, is an impossibility; in fact, the opposite is almost certain.

Ice Ages probably come about when the tilt of the earth's axis changes, or when clouds of interstellar dust drift through the solar system, blocking some of the light from the sun. No one is sure. However, during the last million years there have been cycles of glacial growth. Glaciers have advanced and retreated many times, and no doubt will again.

Yet for all that might happen, the weather will, no doubt, be only somewhat worse. However, even if some areas return to deserts and others are flooded by the seas, no terrible disasters are in sight. Mankind can survive a great deal. People can leave deserts or flooded cities. They can move, with art treasures and other valuable possessions, northward to wetter, cooler climates. They can live in much worse conditions, including another Ice Age. After all, our ancestors lived through an Ice Age, even though they had no decent clothing, no furnaces, no well-built houses. If they could do it, the people of the future can do it.

Weather will not be the problem so much as pollution, as environmental destruction. So our generation, which has inherited the wonderful earth, must take better care of it.

Index

About the Author

Howard Smith is the author of over twenty books for children and adults, including many on the natural and physical sciences. His most recent books include *Small Worlds* and *Daring the Unknown: A History of NASA.* Having been caught in the great hurricane of 1938 and a Wyoming blizzard with winds of 125 miles an hour, he has a keen interest in the subject of weather. Mr. Smith has lived in many places in the United States, but now lives in New York City with his wife.

About the Illustrator

Jeffrey Bedrick studied film at San Francisco State University and studied art privately with Gage Taylor. He has worked as commercial and fine artist and his works have been exhibited extensively in California. He lives in Marin County, California.

CIRRUS

CIRROCUMULUS

CIRROSTRATUS

ALTOCUMULUS

ALTOSTRATUS